ACE place!

Toilets
in history

BY
ELIZABETH NEWBERY

A & C BLACK
AN IMPRINT OF BLOOMSBURY
LONDON OXFORD NEW YORK NEW DELHI SYDNEY

First published in 1999 by
A & C Black, an imprint of Bloomsbury Publishing Plc
50 Bedford Square, London WC1B 3DP
www.bloomsbury.com

Bloomsbury is a registered trademark of Bloomsbury Publishing Plc

Written by Elizabeth Newbery
Researched by Rachel Minay and John Rhodes
Designed by Nicole Griffin
Illustrated by Graham Cox
Created by Newbery & England

A CIP record for this book is available from the British Library.

ISBN 978-0-7136-5152-2

This book is produced using paper that is made from wood grown
in managed, sustainable forests. It is natural, renewable and
recyclable. The logging and manufacturing processes conform
to the environmental regulations of the country of origin.

The publishers are grateful for permission to reproduce the following:
p.4, 6, 8 © English Heritage; p.11 Don Baldwin;
p.13 The Royal Collection © Her Majesty The Queen;
p.15 © Science & Society Picture Library;
p.17 © V&A Picture Library; p.19 © Mary Evans Picture Library;
p.21 © The Robert Opie Collection;
p.23 Beamish: The North of England Open Air Museum.

Printed in China by C&C Offset Printing Co Ltd, Shenzhen, Guangdong

CONTENTS

A SMELLY OLD PROBLEM

Lots of people living together make enormous amounts of waste. Unless it's cleared, sewage spreads disease. Throughout history people have dealt with the pongy problem in different ways. Find out how they solved toilet troubles in crowded cities, captured castles and a splendid royal palace.

I invented the first flush toilet

I planned super sewers for London

We used the netty

Just think how many times a day you use the toilet. Imagine if you couldn't flush the sewage away and it built up into huge piles! Much, much worse – what if the muck wasn't just yours but that of all the people living in your village, town or city?

There are lots of other words for 'toilet': latrine, lavatory, necessary house, bog, bathroom, cloakroom, outhouse, powder room, privy, urinal, garderobe, gents, ladies, public convenience, washroom, water closet, WC, loo, smallest room, sewer, earth closet, netty. Can you think of any more?

How many toilets like this can you find hidden in the book? Find the answer on page 30.

3

KEEN TO BE CLEAN

The Romans were extremely fussy about cleanliness. When the army came to Britain nearly 2000 years ago, they found the Celts didn't have a way of getting rid of sewage. So the Romans built toilets called **LATRINES,** first in their forts and then in towns.

Many hundreds of Roman soldiers were stationed in large forts such as Housesteads along Hadrian's Wall. The latrines had to be well organised because they were so busy!

The latrines at Housesteads were built over deep channels and flushed with rainwater stored in large stone tanks. The sewage was washed away under the fort wall and into a ditch.

The latrines had wooden seats which rotted away long ago. There were eight seats on each side.

In towns, Roman men and women went to the toilet together. The public latrines had no doors, or walls between each toilet. Everybody could see everyone else. But men and women both wore long robes so nobody could see *exactly* what was going on!

These Roman soldiers used sponge sticks to wipe their bottoms, then they rinsed the sticks in a drain. A slave poured water over the soldiers' hands.

What kind of nut do you find in a loo?

Answer: a peenut!

5

GARDY-LOO!

In the Middle Ages, people in towns lived in **FILTHY CONDITIONS**. Streets were ankle-deep in muck. Rats fed on the rubbish and people suffered from diseases spread by germs in the dirt.

At night, people went to the loo in pots. The next day, they tipped the muck out of the window and cried 'gardy-loo!' to warn people!

What has four wheels and flies?

Gardy-loo!

Over time, people tried to clean up towns. In the 1400s more streets were paved and cleaned, and more public toilets were built. Sir Richard (Dick) Whittington left money to build one in the City of London with 64 seats.

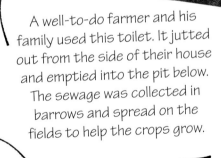

A well-to-do farmer and his family used this toilet. It jutted out from the side of their house and emptied into the pit below. The sewage was collected in barrows and spread on the fields to help the crops grow.

There are lots of stories of people falling through rotten wooden floors into pits and drowning in the sludge!

Answer: a rubbish cart!

DANGEROUS DUNG

astles needed well-organised ways of getting rid of sewage and other rubbish. If a castle was surrounded by attackers and there was no way of clearing the muck, it would pile up and the defenders would die of horrible **DISEASES.**

What do you call a lady with two toilets?

To solve the problem of disease, toilets called garderobes were built into the thickness of a castle's walls. The sewage fell down chutes straight into the moat. Fish in the moat fed on the waste. But if there was no moat, the sewage emptied into a pit which had to be cleaned out by hand!

Castle builders had to make sure that garderobes were well protected. Once, a castle in France was captured when attackers climbed up the large garderobe chutes!

This garderobe chute at Longtown Castle in Herefordshire has a large opening. But it is high up on the castle wall so attackers would find it difficult to reach.

Urine contains ammonia which is used in the curing of leather. Old pee was collected from castles and other places where lots of people lived and sold to leather-workers!

Answer: Lulu

9

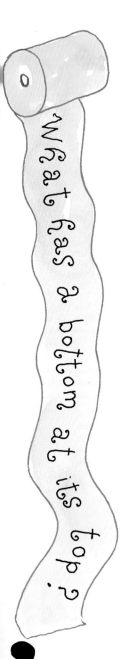

What has a bottom at its top?

The monks who lived at Mount Grace Priory, Yorkshire, lived alone in their own tiny houses. They each had a toilet like this one.

The monks called a toilet a 'necessary house'. It comes from the Latin word **NECESSARIUM**, which means toilet. The word 'lavatory' comes from the Latin word **LAVATORIUM**. This was the place where monks washed their hands before or after eating.

CLEAN HABITS

In the Middle Ages the best toilets were in religious houses. Big monasteries and nunneries housed hundreds of monks or nuns, so they needed huge blocks of toilets. These were built in a special part of the monastery called the **REREDORTER**. But the toilets weren't built for comfort – lingering in lavatories wasn't allowed!

Monasteries often had very good water systems. In 1349, the Black Death struck the country. But super-clean drains at Christchurch monastery in Canterbury kept the monks safe from the killer disease.

Separate toilet

Wooden seat

Muck dropped down a chute

Monks used branches from trees to clear blocked pipes.

In the Middle Ages, these toilets at Rievaulx Abbey were considered luxurious!

Muck was washed away by a stream

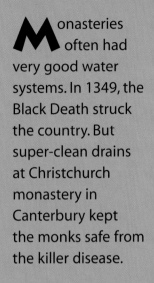

Answer: a leg!

In some royal palaces the toilets emptied into pits. They were scrubbed out by special workers called gong scourers. It was so dark, they had to work by candlelight. For much of Henry VIII's reign, the royal scourer was Philip Long. He had a team of boys or small men who climbed inside the pits.

A ROYAL LOO

Hampton Court Palace, near London, was one of Henry VIII's palaces. Grand courtiers and humble servants all shared the same **HUGE TOILET**. It could seat 14 people at a time. The sewage emptied into drains which ran under the palace moat and then into the River Thames that flowed through London.

What did one eye say to the other?

What a pong!

Henry VIII had a very special toilet called a close-stool. When Henry used it, a servant called the 'Groom of the Stole' would be on hand with a basin, jug, towel and a cloth to wipe the royal bottom. He also had to empty the potty and get rid of any horrible smells.

A portable box with a hinged lid

A padded seat

A metal potty inside

You can see this close-stool at Hampton Court Palace. It is padded with crimson velvet and trimmed with ribbon and gilt studs. Henry's close-stool must have been very like this one.

Answer: there's something between us that smells!

13

PULL THE CHAIN

In 1449 Thomas Brightfield invented a type of toilet that was flushed by water from a water tank called a **CISTERN**. The idea was too far ahead of its time and didn't catch on for years.

The next person to develop the idea of a flushing toilet was Sir John Harington, godson of Queen Elizabeth I. In 1596 he made a toilet which let the muck out of the bottom of the pan. At the same time, it released a flush of water from the cistern above. Elizabeth I used the toilet and liked it so much that she had one made for Richmond Palace.

What did Queen Elizabeth I do when she made a bad smell?

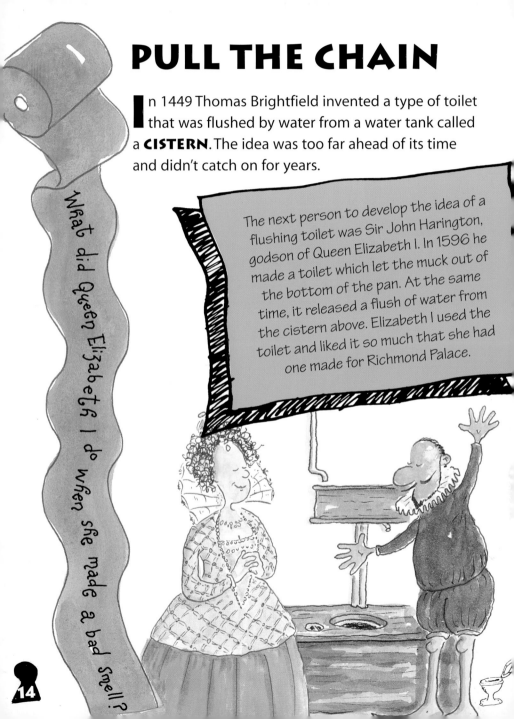

The next great advance was made by Alexander Cummings in 1775. His toilet had a special sliding part to let the sewage flush out. It also had a soil pipe bent into an 'S' to stop the smell coming back up from below. It was called a stink trap!

This was the design for Alexander Cummings' flushing toilet.

Then Joseph Bramah improved on Alexander's ideas. In 1778 he developed a toilet that flushed everything away by opening a valve, and let in fresh water by another valve. Later, an engineer called Rogers Field improved the idea again. His toilet allowed the right amount of water to be released without wasting any. But a flushing loo inside a house was a luxury for most people until the 20th century.

Bramah's toilet looked like this. You pulled the handle up to empty the pan. The handle was connected to a wire which opened a valve in the cistern. Water flushed down the pipe and cleaned the pan.

Answer: she issued a royal pardon!

Sewage and rubbish were collected from cesspits in special carts by 'night-soil' men. They worked at night because there were fewer smells and flies in the cool air. Night-soil men often worked as chimney sweeps during the day.

A TERRIBLE PONG

By the 1700s many people living in cities had a deep pit for burying waste (called a cesspit) in their garden or under their house. The smell was horrible even in the best houses. There were lots of scary stories about people dying mysteriously of the 'night air'. Today we know that the deadly killer was a mix of **POISONOUS GASES**.

Why did the scientist hide under the bed ?

In the 1700s babies had their nappies changed only once a day and they were trained to use a potty as soon as they were a few weeks old. Most children suffered with stomach pains and diarrhoea so often that the potty had to be close at hand!

Some babies had a potty fitted in a chair called a commode. You can see this one at the Bethnal Green Museum of Childhood in London. The baby was probably strapped in.

Adults used potties too! They were kept in the bedroom - and in the dining room. Gentlemen used them after dinner, once the ladies had left the room.

Answer: because he thought he was a little potty!

THE BIG STINK

In Victorian times, big cities became overcrowded. Working people lived in tiny houses all crammed together and they shared an outside toilet called a **PRIVY**. Sometimes, more than 100 people shared the same one! The privies could not cope with all the waste and it overflowed into the streets and rivers.

In 1858 a heatwave caused the filthy River Thames to stink worse than ever. The smell was so bad that MPs in the Houses of Parliament demanded to meet elsewhere.

In the same year as the Big Stink, the Government asked an engineer called Sir Joseph Bazalgette to build a new sewer system for London. Over 83 miles of sewers were built to carry 420 million gallons of water every day. The sewers were completed in 1865 and soon the number of people dying of killer diseases began to fall.

In London, sewage, dead animals, waste from slaughter-houses and breweries, horse dung, and chemicals from factories were all dumped straight into the Thames. People drank the same water! So, deadly diseases such as cholera and typhoid fever were common. In the 1830s an attack of cholera killed tens of thousands of people in Britain.

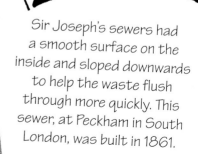

Sir Joseph's sewers had a smooth surface on the inside and sloped downwards to help the waste flush through more quickly. This sewer, at Peckham in South London, was built in 1861.

Answer: pollution!

19

LUXURIOUS LAVATORIES

After 1850, inventors and engineers developed ways of piping **HOT, RUNNING WATER** into houses. For the first time, wealthy people could have bathrooms and toilets with a plumbed water supply. Many poor families could not afford these luxuries for another 100 years.

When Queen Victoria travelled by train, she expected the same standard of comfort as she had in her palaces and castles. So she had her own, special railway carriage with a commode inside it, just for her!

Sir William Armstrong was a wealthy inventor and arms dealer who lived at Cragside, a huge house in Northumberland. Cragside had the best bathroom and lavatory for miles around. It had hot and cold plunge baths, a shower, a cool room, a steam room and a lavatory, all decorated with beautiful Turkish tiles.

Why didn't the millionair

Darling, I must have one!

Thomas Crapper started a plumbing business in Chelsea, London, in 1861. He made some of the best designed toilets around. Many of his designs were put in public conveniences, hotels, factories and schools as well as private houses. You can still see many of them today.

Lavatorie

MADE · IN · ROYAL "C.V." Porcelain WHITE or IVORY.

COMBINATION No 107.   £10 0 0.

People could buy toilets from catalogues. This toilet was called 'The Deluge'. It was made by Thomas Crapper and Company and cost just under £4.

have any toilets in his mansion?

NIPPING TO THE NETTY

If you lived in the countryside in Victorian times you might have used a privy called an **EARTH CLOSET**. This was really just a hole in a plank set over a bucket. Each time someone used the privy, they covered the sewage with a layer of earth. When the bucket was full, the contents were spread on the garden or on the fields nearby, along with other farmyard manure.

People still use outside 'privies' on building sites and boats, and at country shows, pop festivals in fields or other places where there are no permanent toilets. But instead of earth or ashes, chemicals break down the waste.

In the North of England, a privy was called a 'netty'. People tipped ash from fireplaces and nearby coke furnaces on top of the sewage to stop it smelling. The ash and muck mixture was cleared out of a trapdoor and used to grow prize leeks and onions!

A vicar called Henry Moule decided to put the ash and muck waste to the test. He persuaded a farmer to fertilise half a field with the muck from his earth closet and the other half with artificial fertilisers. The farmer planted swedes in both halves of the field. The swedes planted in manure from the earth closet grew three times as big!

CLEAN BOTTOMS

So what did people use to wipe their **BOTTOMS**? Remember - in the past there was no soft toilet paper!

In earliest times people squatted in fields and used leaves, moss, stones or clumps of grass.

In the Middle Ages monks and nuns living in monasteries used rags. Other people used oyster or mussel shells, bits of broken pots or bunches of herbs. Wealthy ladies were said to have used goose feathers because they were nice and soft.

What do you call two policemen?

The Romans had a goddess of sewers called Venus Cloacina. Public toilets were called **CLOACA**, which is where we get 'cloakroom' from.

Monks ate buckthorn berries to make them go to the toilet more easily.

In the 1700s, you could pay for the services of a human toilet in Edinburgh. A man carrying a bucket hid you under a cloak while you went to the loo.

How do astronauts go to the loo? Spacecraft such as Skylab have toilets with handles that they grip to stop themselves floating off. Astronauts (both men and women) pee into a funnel attached to waste pipes. The pee is dumped in space. Astronauts working outside spacecraft wear very absorbent pants under their space suits.

Answer: a pair of navy blue knickers!

The first toilet paper was sold in 1880 by the British Perforated Paper Company. Today you can buy patterned and perfumed toilet paper in all kinds of colours!

HERE'S ONE
I MADE EARLIER

In 1204, Chateau Gaillard in France was captured by attackers who climbed up the garderobe chutes. Make this garderobe out of card and watch a soldier pop out from the chute!

You will need:
* card
* stiff paper
* a piece of card measuring about 12 cm x 12 cm
* strong glue and a spreader
* tracing paper
* a craft knife
* a ruler • felt tips

What to do:

1 Trace the lid and base patterns on p. 27 onto card. Use the craft knife and ruler to score along the dotted fold lines. (Be careful not to cut through!)

2 Cut out the lid and base patterns and the slots. Fold the lid along the dotted line, folding up the lid towards you. Then fold the flaps away from you. Push the shaft through slot A so that just the round lid shape pokes out.

3 Trace the soldier pattern onto the stiff paper and cut it out. Fold the glue tab back and stick it to the glue tab on the lid pattern. Push the bottom of the soldier through slot B.

4 Fold the base pattern along the dotted lines so that it makes a box shape. Dab glue onto tab A and B and stick to your square piece of card. Colour the soldier to make him look really mucky.

5 Pull the arrow and watch the soldier pop out of the garderobe!

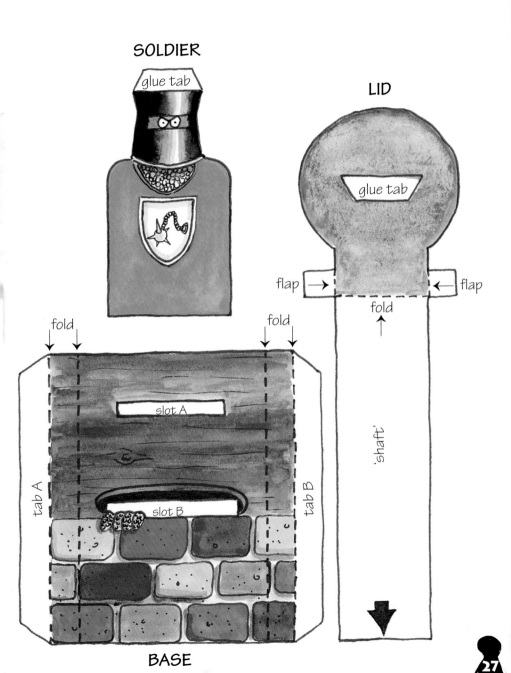

SOLDIER

glue tab

LID

glue tab

flap → ← flap

fold

fold fold

fold

tab A

slot A

'shaft'

slot B

tab B

BASE

27

ON THE TRACK OF TOILETS

Pages 4-5

You can find one of the best preserved Roman military latrines in Europe at **HOUSESTEADS ROMAN FORT** on Hadrian's Wall in Northumberland. You can also see the remains of latrines in the fort hospital and in the commandant's house. The fort is in the care of English Heritage. The address is Housesteads Museum, Haydon Bridge, Hexham, Northumberland, NE47 6NN Tel: 01434 344363.

Pages 6-7

Look out for a garderobe in **BAYLEAF FARMHOUSE** in the Weald and Downland Open Air Museum in West Sussex. Have a go at sitting in it! Weald and Downland Open Air Museum, Singleton, West Sussex PO18 OEU Tel: 01243 811363.

Pages 8-9

LONGTOWN CASTLE is in Herefordshire and entry is free! You can find garderobes in most castles in the care

of English Heritage. Tel: 020 7973 3434 for more information about the castle and other English Heritage Sites.

BEAUMARIS CASTLE in Anglesey, North Wales has garderobe chutes shaped like faces. The waste fell out through the mouths! In Wales, many castles are in the care of Cadw. Tel: 01248 810361 for more information.

Historic Scotland looks after **CASTLES IN SCOTLAND.** Tel: 0131 668 8600 for information about castles.

Pages 10-11

You can explore a reredorter at **RIEVAULX ABBEY**, near Helmsley, North Yorkshire YO6 5LB tel: 01439 798228. There are more toilets to discover at **MOUNT GRACE PRIORY**, Staddle Bridge, Northallerton, North Yorkshire DL6 3JG tel: 01609 883494. Rievaulx Abbey and Mount Grace Priory are both in the care of English Heritage.

Pages 12-13

You can find a close-stool in the King's Apartment at **HAMPTON COURT PALACE**, East Molesey, Surrey KT8 9AU tel: 0844 482 7777.

You can find another close-stool at **KNOLE**, near Sevenoaks, Kent TN15 ORP tel: 01732 450608. Knole is in the care of the National Trust.

Pages 14-15
The **SCIENCE MUSEUM** has a good selection on toilets. The Science Museum is on Exhibition Road, London SW7 2DD tel: 0870 8704868.

Pages 16-17
Many houses owned by the National Trust have interesting toilets and commodes, including **BERRINGTON HALL,** near Leominster, Herefordshire HR6 ODW tel: 01568 615721; CASTLE DROGO, near Exeter, Devon EX6 6PB tel: 01647 433306; **KNIGHTSHAYES COURT**, near Tiverton, Devon EX16 7RQ; tel: 01884 254665; and **BLICKLING HALL,** Norwich NR11 6NF tel: 01263 738030.

You can find an early nappy and a child's commode at the **BETHNAL GREEN MUSEUM OF CHILDHOOD**, Cambridge Heath Rd, London E2 9PA tel: 020 8983 5200.

Pages 20-21
You can wander through the Turkish bathroom at **CRAGSIDE HOUSE,** Rothbury, Morpeth Northumberland NE65 7PX tel: 01669 620333. It is owned by the National Trust.

Look out for Queen Victoria's commode in the royal train at the **NATIONAL RAILWAY MUSEUM,** Leeman Road, York YO6 4XJ tel: 08448 153139

Pages 22-23
Find a netty at the **BEAMISH OPEN AIR MUSEUM,** Co Durham DH9 ORG tel: 0191 3704000; a privy at **BLISTS HILL VICTORIAN TOWN,** Madeley, Telford tel: 01952 586063, and in the toll house garden at the **WEALD AND DOWNLAND OPEN AIR MUSEUM** (see above).

Pages 24-25
You can find examples of early toilet paper at the **ROBERT OPIE COLLECTION MUSEUM OF BRANDS, PACKAGING AND ADVERTISING**, 2 Colville Mews, Lonsdale Road, London W11 2AR tel: 020 7908 0880.

INDEX

There are 15 hidden toilets. They are on pages 4, 5, 7, 9, 11, 13, 14, 15, 16, 17, 18, 21, 22, 24 and 25.